For the Love of Buddy

A Heartfelt Tale About the Journey of a Girl and Her Cat

By **Dyanna Morrison**

Illustrations by **Mike Motz**

ISBN: 979-8-9852538-1-8 (hardcover)
ISBN: 979-8-9852538-0-1 (paperback)
ISBN: 979-8-9852538-2-5 (ebook)

Copyright © 2002, 2021 by Dyanna Morrison White

All rights reserved. This book may not be reproduced in whole or in part,
in any form or by any means, electronic or mechanical, including photocopying,
recording or by any information storage and retrieval system now known
or hereafter invented, without written permission from the Author/Publisher.

**To Buddy - You will always hold
a forever place in my heart**

**And to Maddie, Winston, Auggie, Cooper,
and Winston II for a lifetime of memories.
How lucky I have been to be your "Cat Mom"**

**"What greater gift than the love of a cat?"
Charles Dickens**

Seventeen years ago
In a town full of snow
Samantha, my cat, had some kittens.
One was a boy who acted quite coy
With a purr like a roar – I was smitten!

So I made him my mister,
And our journey in life then got started.
It was long and eventful
With memories – a tent-full!
All for the love of Buddy.

We left the hometown
And journeyed Rhode Island bound
To start a new life near the ocean.

With pollens in the breezes,
poor Buddy got wheezing and sneezing
And had to curtail from his mousing.
But a doctor's shrewd notion delivered a potion,
And his asthma was cured – what a breakthrough!

It would often be fun as he basked in the sun
To wonder of what he was dreaming…
Of cheeses from Paris and roast beef, the rarest!
As he lazily stretched floor to ceiling
With sides of Maine lobster and cream by the potful
All for the love of Buddy.

A manly man's cat
He was never one that
Went for fancy manicures or grooming.
With a few hairs astray
He looked handsome that way!
All for the love of Buddy.

A hunter by night
It was truly a fright, to see
what he'd bring home by daylight.
No prey was too quick for him to outwit
With a leap and a lunge he'd win outright!

And with a sheepish grin,
he would bring them right in
And I'd try to admonish his prowess.
Then he'd give me that look,
I'd give in, I was hooked!
All for the love of Buddy.

Then many years passed in our old East side flat.

They were happy years full of contentment.

In his favorite blue chair, he was pure "laissez-faire."

As he daydreamed, I'd watch with attachment.

With purrs through the day's fold,

We were happy to grow old!

All for the love of Buddy.

My friends would come over
For fine wine and clover.
We'd sit and spend hours a talking.
And he'd climb up to greet us
And sit in between us
As he rightfully soaked up attention.
The star of the show
My only hero.
All for the love of Buddy.

As the years moseyed on
We decided upon
Returning to visit the hometown.
His laid back way and big belly, they say
Brought on sugar diabetes.
Two injections a day took his big thirst away
And everything got back to normal.
Spry and amazing,
Nothing could phase him!
All for the love of Buddy.

Then after years of scheming
and California dreaming
Destiny called on the tele.
So I packed up a van with fine carpets, so grand!
To ensure Buddy's comfort in transit.
He sat in the back like a cool West coast cat!
All for the love of Buddy.

Cross the country we drove,
Through the states we did roam,
As we got closer to our destination.

He was strictly first class.

Only Chilean Sea Bass

His request from room service for dinner.

As he sipped heavy cream – the American dream!

All for the love of Buddy.

If I could, I would give him the sun and the moon
And warm rubs on his cheek which he loved so!
And he'd kiss me right back, nothing's better than that!
With a purr and a double-winked head nod,

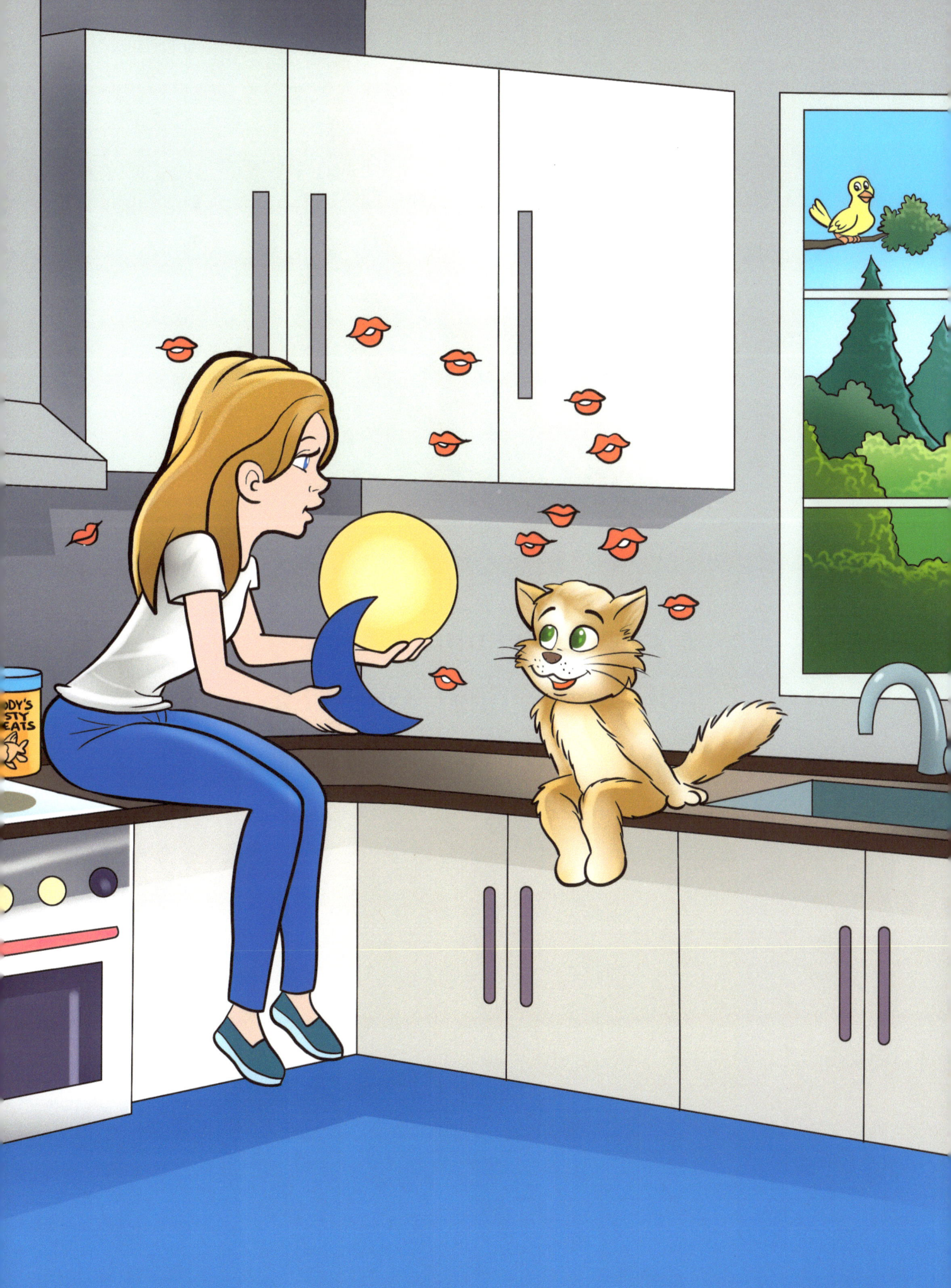

And crawl under the covers
Till dawn's light would hover.
All for the love of Buddy.

Then one warm summer's day,
Buddy's strength went away.
It was time for my friend to be leaving.
Through my tears I concurred, and that day is a blur.
I just wasn't prepared for the grieving!
For how do you say goodbye to a friend
Who has brought you such joy and contentment?

You kiss his fine head as he lay on the bed
And give thanks for the years that were God-sent!
And you know you were blessed
So you lay him to rest.
All for the love of Buddy.

I miss you, dear friend,
So with much love I send
This heartfelt abundance of wishes!
I wish you a rainbow
And tuna – a train-full!
With love that transcends
I know you're with me, my friend!
As you watch over me from the Heavens,
I'd climb up to meet you!
With kisses – a beach-full
All for the love of Buddy.

About the Author

Dyanna has spent the majority of her adult life in either Providence, RI, or San Diego, CA. An award-winning writer, in 2020-2021, Dyanna released *Justice*, the first book/stage play in the Justice trilogy. She also recently released *Liberty*, the second book/stage play in the trilogy.

A lifelong lover of cats, Buddy was her beloved companion for almost seventeen years that went by all too quickly! She wrote this poem to honor their journey in life together. Sadly, Dyanna recently lost other members of her furry family and has also completed, *For the Love of Winston*, which will be the next book she releases.

Dyanna currently lives in Providence, RI, with her two tuxedo cats, Cooper and Winston II. She enjoys the beach, gardening, Pilates, cooking, history, and writing.